STEPPING
Stones
Walking Lake Michigan

Written by Carol Trembath
Illustrated by David W. Craig

Dedication

THIS BOOK IS DEDICATED TO Grandmother Josephine Mandamin, an Anishinaabe (Ojibway) member and founder of the Mother Earth Water Walkers.

Many years ago Josephine saw that our precious water was in trouble. Water was being polluted and siphoned away. She took up the challenge given to her by the Grand Chief of the Three Fires Midewiwin Lodge when he asked, "What are you going to do about it?"

With the Great Lakes at the heart of the historical Anishinaabe territory, Josephine decided to draw attention to the condition of water by walking the perimeter of each of the Great Lakes. In the spring of 2003, Josephine and a group of supporters began their first water walk by circling Lake Superior. Since then water from lakes, rivers, and even oceans has been carried in copper pails over countless roads in an effort to show others the importance of protecting the water.

Today Josephine's message continues to send out ripples and waves to communities across the Midwest and beyond. There is an ever-widening circle of concerned citizens and civic leaders who are exploring a new vision for water—one that ensures a sustainable future for all of Earth's living inhabitants.

With every step there has been a growing certainty within Josephine regarding her mission, but she felt some concern over my endeavor to write children's books about the Water Walkers story. She shared her uneasiness when she wrote to me, saying:

"I have had misgivings about what you are doing. Many offerings have been made for an answer to my misgivings. In our culture we tell oral teachings or draw. In your culture, it is different. To that I give my respect. I have pondered on the reason why you are doing this. I pondered about ego, money, fame. What is it she wants, I asked? Finally, the response came:

'It is for the Water. Simple—for the water.'

"I give my blessings for the water. Now I can rest easy."

Both Josephine's real life story and Mai's adventure with her grandmother in this book, *Stepping Stones*, speak to the heart and soul of this nation. We are all one and part of the Great Circle. Josephine is moving forward to build a deeper awareness of water and of the impact of American culture on the environment.

When asked why she is doing this, she replied, "We are not doing this for ourselves, we're doing this for you. What will you tell your grandchildren when they ask, *what did you do for the water?*"

Follow your own stepping stones and find the spirit of water...
—Carol Trembath

"This we know. The earth does not belong to man; man belongs to earth. This we know. All things are connected like the blood which unites one family. All things are connected. Whatever befalls the earth befalls the sons of the earth. Man did not weave the web of life; he is merely a strand in it. Whatever he does to the web, he does to himself..."
–Chief Seattle

"The human brain now holds the key to our future. We have to recall the image of the planet from outer space; a single entity in which air, water, and continents are interconnected. That is our home."
—David Suzuki

Acknowledgements

"*One finger cannot lift a pebble.*" – Hopi proverb

"*It takes a thousand voices to tell a single story.*" – Native American proverb

A book is never the solitary work of a writer. One always stands on the shoulders of all who taught, encouraged, and cheered the writer on. Many associates worked on this story and added to its energy namely, David W. Craig, illustrator; Streetlight Graphics, graphic designer; Linda McLean, and my family who listened countless times to the story and offered insights. Stepping Stones stands on the incredible story of the Mother Earth Water Walkers and their determined leader—Josephine Mandamin.

To all—Chi Miigwetch.

Stepping Stones

Copyright © 2017 by Carol Trembath

All rights reserved. Except as permitted under U.S. Copyright Act of 1976, no part of this publication may be reproduced, distributed, or transmitted in any form or by any means, or stored in a database or retrieval system, without the prior written permission of the publisher.

ISBN 13: 978-0-9907446-4-1
ISBN 10: 0-9907446-4-7

Library of Congress Control Number: 2017901217

Illustrations by David W. Craig

Lakeside Publishing MI

Printed in the United States of America

About the Water Walkers

THE MOTHER EARTH WATER WALKERS began their journey in 2003 when Native women walked 1,372 miles around Lake Superior. In 2004, 2005, 2006, and 2007 the Mother Earth Water Walkers encircled Lake Michigan, Huron, Ontario and Erie respectfully. In 2008 the Water Walkers revisited Lake Michigan. In 2009 Lake Ontario was circled from Kingston, Ontario to the Atlantic Ocean along the St. Lawrence River.

Beyond the Great Lakes area, the Mother Earth Water Walkers walked down rivers including the Mississippi River in 2013 and the Ohio River in 2014. In 2011 Native People walked from the four directions: from the Atlantic, Pacific, Hudson Bay, and the Gulf of Mexico and came together to pour the healing waters of the oceans into Lake Superior. In 2015 they walked from Quebec to Madeline Island and in 2017 they walked from Duluth, Minnesota to Quebec. For the past fourteen years they have walked over 18,500 miles to call attention to the sacred gift of water.

The Ojibway (or Chippewa), Ottawa (or Odawa) and Potawatomi were known by Native tradition, as the "Council of Three Fires." According to Naïve tradition, the Ojibway were the caretakers of the Eastern Woodlands and the Great Lakes. The Anishinabek women as givers-of-life were responsible for speaking for, protecting, and carrying the water. Their walk with a copper pail of water was a way of walking the talk. Walking, the slowest form on transportation, reinforced an ancient value of taking a public stand. Each of the steps was a prayer for the water, Mother Earth, animals, birds, insects, trees, and the human family.

Turtle Island is the name of North America according to many indigenous people. Approximately 300-400 years ago Native people began migrating westward away from the eastern section of North America. Where tribes stopped were called *"stepping stones"* or small turtle islands. The places they stopped are today called: Montreal, Niagara Falls, Detroit, Manitoulin Island, Sault Ste. Marie, Duluth and Madeline Island. The story *Stepping Stones* is a reminder of Native People's ongoing endurance and task of protecting Mother Earth.

Lake Michigan was the location of the second water walk which began near Manistee. Lake Michigan's name is derived from the Algonquin word *Michigami* meaning "great water". The central character in the story is Mai. Her name means coyote and coyote is a teacher in Native folklore.

The following is a children's fiction story. It is a tribute to the Native women and men who have walked countless miles to draw attention to the condition of water. It is an "imaginary version" that describes what many dedicated and courageous indigenous people have done to protect and preserve water for generations to come. If you would like to learn more about the Mother Earth Water Walkers, go to their website at motherearthwaterwalk.com.

Swish, swish, swish. Water swirled in the copper pail. *Pa-tump, pa-tump, pa-tump.* My tired feet pounded on the roadside path. But my grandfather's memory bag felt soft and light against my skin. I remembered how Grandmother hung it around my neck the night before we left.

She said, "Mai, you can put special things in it on our water walk. We will walk to raise awareness of how important it is to take care of the water. We will circle the lakes to protect them for our children and grandchildren. This year we will travel the path of our ancestors around Lake Michigan."

The next morning, long before sunrise, we met up with my brother Kip, my Uncle Joe, my sister Winona, and others from our Ojibway tribe.

The sun was hot and the road was dusty. Sometimes I walked with my grandmother or rested in the van. Other times I helped Kip look for bottles and cans to recycle. I knew it was another way for us to take care of the water. "Here's another bottle," I'd shout.

Each day we walked past towns and forests. I smelled the green pine trees. I heard the chirping of birds and saw the fluttering of butterflies. Every morning before our daily walk, my job was to pour the lake water into the copper pail. We then prayed and sang Ojibway healing songs to bless the water. We left tobacco as a gift of thanks.

We went north along the big lake's shoreline past the Sleeping Bear Dunes. Sometimes I walked barefoot on the beach. I dashed in and out of the waves. When no one was looking, I winked and waved at the big lake and it shimmered and waved back at me.

Near Glen Arbor, Grandmother handed me a pearly-white stone from the beach. "This is a moonstone," she said. "It is to remind you of Grandmother Moon. Your spirit is like the twinkling moon. It reflects back to us a soft, sweet light."

"Thank you, Grandmother. I think Grandmother Moon talks with her daughter, Mother Earth, like you talk to me."

Grandmother smiled, "Yes, Mai. I think she does." I put the moonstone in my memory bag.

As we walked with our eagle staff and copper pail, cars slowed down to look at us. One morning a car stopped and the driver rolled down his window.

"Go back to your reservation," he shouted. "You don't belong here." Then someone from the back seat threw something. Tomatoes splashed on the Water Walkers. Red juice streamed down Grandmother's face.

"I don't want to walk anymore, Grandmother," I said. "I don't want someone to hurt you."

"Mai, don't let the actions of others frighten you. We belong here."

"But those people scared me!"

"Mai, sometimes when we cross a stream, we use stepping stones. You might want to use words to be your stepping stones. I will tell you an Ojibway story." Grandmother put a small rock in my hand. It was round and green.

"Grandmother, I love looking for rocks, but this stone looks just like a turtle shell."

"It's called a *green stone*." said Grandmother.

"Our ancestors believed that we live on the back of a Great Turtle. A turtle carries its home on its back. It cannot separate itself from its home. Just like the turtle, we cannot separate ourselves from our home—Mother Earth. She will care for us as long as we care for her."

"Grandmother, if we're walking on the Great Turtle, won't we fall off?"

Grandmother laughed, "No, Mai, you won't fall off. Mother Earth is very big."

The stories of my people made me feel better. Soon we climbed in canoes and crossed the Grand Traverse Bay. The water was deep and big waves splashed the canoe. When we landed, I found a gray stone with white circles. Winona asked Uncle Joe, "Isn't that a Petoskey stone?"

"Yes," he said. "It is the skeletal remains of coral that lived millions of years ago. Even the smallest creatures leave their mark on Mother Earth." I wondered to myself what marks I was leaving behind.

"Grandmother look. I found these brown rocks on the beach. Uncle Joe said they came from beneath the waves. He called them lightning rocks. He said these scratchy, white lines look like lightning hit them.

But watch me. I am going to hit them together." Crack, Crack, Crack. "Grandmother, did you hear it? Did you hear the thunder?"

"I think I did, Mai."

"I am calling them talking rocks because they look like they have little pictures on them. They can help me tell stories."

"You might tell a story about this journey," smiled Grandmother.

I felt the stones in my memory bag. They were rough or smooth. Each had a story to tell about Mother Earth. "Grandmother, I will remember the glow of the moonstone, the turtle of the green stone, the fossils of the Petoskey stones, and the picture-stories of the lightning rock."

"I want to walk with you around the other Great Lakes and learn more about Mother Earth."

"Yes, Mai. You might want to tell others about what you are seeing through your words and stories."

"I will, Grandmother. I promise."

Words to Know

Anishinaabe – A member of indigenous people (usually called aboriginal in Canada or First Nations), many of whom live in the U.S. states of Michigan, Wisconsin, and Minnesota, and in Canada in the provinces of Quebec, Ontario, Manitoba, and Saskatchewan.

Biodegradable – Materials that can be broken down by natural processes and absorbed harmlessly into the environment.

Climate change – A measurable change in the climate, temperature, and weather patterns, in the Earth that many scientists believe to be the result of global warming.

Conservation – The protection of animals, plants, and natural resources.

Council of Three Fires – A long-standing Anishinabek alliance of the Ojibway (or Chippewa), Ottawa (or Odawa), and Potawatomi tribes of North America.

Eagle Staff – The eagle staff is a highly honored and sacred object. It commonly looks like a shepherd's staff and is wrapped in either otter or buffalo skin. It displays eagle feathers. In Native traditions it is said that eagles communicate with Creator. The eagle staff, in turn, becomes a conduit for prayer.

Elders – An older influential member of a family, tribe, or community.

Environment – The conditions that surrounds someone or something that affects its growth, health, and/or progress; the natural world around us.

Fossil fuels – Energy sources such as oil, coal, and natural gas that come from the remains (fossils) of living things from the past. Fossil fuels are burned to produce most of the world's energy.

Four Directions – Native people see the world as having four directions. From the four directions, come the four winds. Each direction has a special meaning and color associated with it.

Global warming – An increase of the average temperature of the Earth's atmosphere that many scientists consider to be the cause of adverse effects such as climate change, melting polar ice caps, decreasing air quality, and rising sea levels.

Greenhouse effect – The process by which gases that accumulate high in the Earth's atmosphere trap heat from the sun, hold it, and bounce it back to Earth. This causes a warming effect upon the Earth's surface, oceans, and atmosphere, similar to what happens inside a garden greenhouse keeping plants warm throughout the winter.

Hibernate – To be in a dormant or inactive state during a cold period, especially during the winter.

Indigenous – Existing, growing, or produced naturally in a particular region or environment.

Landfill – A dumping area, either above or under the ground where large amounts of waste are deposited.

Midewiwin – A society created by Native people tribes to share and protect the songs, ceremonies, and sacred teachings of and for the Anishinabek people.

Ozone – A form of oxygen high in the atmosphere that protects the Earth from ultraviolet rays of the sun.

Pollution – Harmful or poisonous substances that are released into the air or water supply.

Recycling – The process of reusing materials that would otherwise be thrown away. Recycling saves energy, helps conserve the world's forests, and reduces waste and landfills.

Three sisters – The three main agricultural crops of various Native American groups in North America: winter squash, maize (corn), and climbing beans.

Turtle Island – The Anishinaabe name for the North American continent.

Water cycle – The continuous, natural process by which water evaporates from bodies of water, collects in the atmosphere as vapor, condenses in clouds, falls to the ground as rain, and evaporates again.

Water pollution – The addition of harmful substances such as fertilizers, pesticides, sewage, oil, or toxic waste to natural water.

Cross-Curriculum Activities

Literacy Connections:
- Read: *The Legend of the Petoskey Stone* by Kathy-jo Wargin.
- Choose one of the four stones described in Stepping Stones (Petoskey stone, greenstone, moonstone, or lightning rock) and write a legend about how these rocks came to be.
- Descriptive Writing – Write a vivid description of your rock. Use the description when playing the Treasure Hunt game as described in the art section.
- Using your "Pet Rock", write a description of what your pet rock can do.
- Using your "Rock Star" as a prompt, form a band with your classmates and write about each one as "rock legends". What rockers are in your rock band?

Science:
- Shoe Box Collection of rocks and minerals – https://www.education.com/activity/article/rock-collection/
- Grow a Crystal Garden – http://engineering.oregonstate.edu/momentum/k12/june04/
- Rock Candy – http://pagingfunmums.com/2017/02/06/how-to-make-your-very-own-rock-candy-at-home/
- Build a Volcano and have it erupt for a class demo – http://www.wikihow.com/Make-a-Volcano

Art:
- Study photographs of Ansel Adams or the paintings of Georgia O'Keeffe and Albert Bierstadt.
    - https://www.okeeffemuseum.org/collections/okeeffes-art/
    - http://www.albertbierstadt.org/slideshow.html

  Create shoebox dioramas or paintings of beautiful rock formations such as Pictured Rocks, Michigan Upper Peninsula; Mauna Loa Volcano, Hawaii; Arch Rock, Mackinac Island; Devil's Tower, Wyoming; Grand Canyon, Arizona
- Pet Rocks –
    - History of Pet Rocks https://en.wikipedia.org/wiki/Pet_Rock
    - How To - http://www.ehow.com/how_16373_make-pet-rock.html?ref=Track2&utm_source=IACB2C
- Painted Rocks – Paint messages or images of inspiration on your favorite rock.
- Treasure Hunt – Decorate a rock and hide it on the school playground. Challenge other classes to try to find your rock. Use the descriptive writing activity as part of the game.

- Inukshuks - https://www.youtube.com/watch?v=JD7rAD_S-fE
    - Build Inukhsuks on school grounds - https://www.youtube.com/watch?v=cf25KoI6CnY
- Research Rock Art and create your own art using sand, chalk, rocks, and etching techniques. See - https://en.wikipedia.org/wiki/Rock_art

Reading Connections:
- *A Rock is Lively* – Poetic and beautiful illustrations of the wonder and beauty of rocks. Use as literary springboard for descriptive writing.
- *Everybody Needs A Rock* – A prelude to rock collecting or finding the perfect rock for the art projects that have been cited.
- *If Rocks Could Sing* – Appeals to the right-brained child, this could inspire an art project.
- *If You Find A Rock* - Poetry and imagery for a literacy project.
- *Lake Michigan Rock Pickers Guide* – Factual information regarding seven important questions: What kind of stone is it? How old is it? Where is it from? How did it get here? How did it form? Where can I find it? How can I polish it?
- *The Legend of the Petoskey Stone* - Compare and contrast to Stepping Stones. Why is one a legend, and one is a work of fiction? Can you tell the difference?
- *Make Your Own Inuksuk* – Rock formations that pointed the way for Inuit people of Canada. Make an inuksuk for the school gardens or classroom. Compare the Inuit people to the Anishinabek people.
- *Rocks* – Hard, Soft, Smooth, and Round – Use as instructional book with identification and collecting rocks.
- *Rocks in His Head* – To inspire students to create their own rock collections with labels.
- *Under Michigan* – This book can be used for class, group, or individual dioramas and timelines where students can explain the findings of what's below the surface of the State of Michigan.

School or Family Field Trips:
- Natural Rock Formations (Virtual) – Pictured Rocks UP https://www.youtube.com/watch?v=YFJtwuDWx9w
- Explore Inuksuks – https://www.youtube.com/watch?v=NKQ97rOwBH0
- Virtual – Salt Mines beneath the city of Detroit – http://detroitsalt.com/history/
- Cranbrook Museum of Science

Social Studies Standards Connections:
- Michigan Studies – Gr. 3, Human Systems – Gr. 4, Environment & Society – Gr. 5, Places and Regions – Gr. 6

"Rocks and minerals; the oldest storytellers."

— A.D. Posey

Moonstone is a a variety of feldspar. It was named for its glowing color sheen that resembles the moonlight. It has a pearly and opalesent schiller (German for twinkle) Its irredescnece come from below the stone's surface when light is refracted between layers of minerals. It can be may colors including white, grey, pink, peach, green, and brown. It is Florida's state gem. It was designated as such to commemorate the Moon landings, which took off from the Kennedy Space Center. Despite being Florida's State Gem, it does not occur there natually.

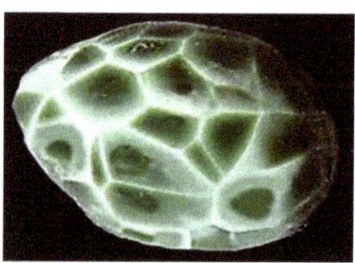

Greenstone - The Michigan State Gem is commonly called "Greenstone" or "Isle Royale Greenstone." The correct mineral name is Chlorastrolite. Michigan residents also refer to it as the "Green Turtle Stone". The name chlorastolite comes from the Green words "chloros" (green) and "astros" (star) which together is "green star stone". This mineral is a green or bluish-green in color and has a pattern of slender, star-like crystals that resembles a "turtle's shell". It was first found in Michigan in in the 1920's in the Keweenaw Peninsula. The best quality greenstones are found on Isle Royale of Michigan where collecting these stones has been prohibited since 2000. Most are small in size with the average size being thumbnail down to pea size. It is usually found as nodules within basalt.

Petoskey stone is a rock and a fossil. It was designated Michigan's state stone in 1965. Petoskey stones have a whitish-gray look when dry and darker gray when wet. The Petoskey stone is a variety of limestone containing an extinct fossilized coral. This "rugose" coral, with its six-sided structure,

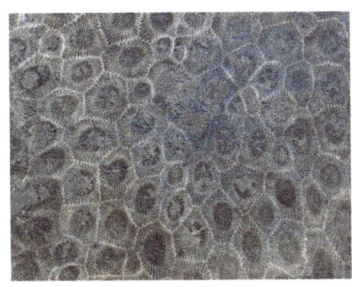
once grew at the bottom on an ancient ocean. During the Devonian time period, what is now Michigan, was near the equator. A warm shallow sea covered the State some 350 million years ago. The stone's name comes from the Indian Chief, Chief Petosegay, which in the Ottawa language means "rays of the rising sun". This six-sided pattern pops up when the rock's surface is wet. Petoskey stones are often found near Petoskey or Charlevoix in the northwest corner of the Michigan's Lower Peninsula.

Lighting Stones are Septarian Nodules. They are found on the beaches in the lower west side of Michigan. They consist of clay cemented into an iron mineral called siderite. They become fractured and the fractures fill with calcite brought in by ground water. The result forms lightning-like patterns on a brown background.

Copper is an element and a mineral. Copper is one of the most famous and useful metals ever since ancient times. Copper is a flexible, reddish metal. In the air it oxides/tarnishes to green. Rock collectors and geologist consider Michigan's Keweenaw Peninsula copper formations the most important copper deposits in the world. The Keweenaw Peninsula is a thumb of land that juts out from the Upper Peninsula of Michigan into Lake Superior. Copper occurs in a wide range of sizes, from sheets several feet across to small nuggets the size of a pea. Copper is an excellent conductor of electricity. The copper mined today is used to conduct electricity, mostly in wiring. It is also an excellent conductor of heat and is used in cooking utensils and building materials. When it comes to famous Michigan rocks and minerals, the Upper Peninsula has copper and the Lower Peninsula has Petoskey stone.

Guthier, Kevin, and Bruce Mueler. *Lake Huron Rock Picker's Guide*. Ann Arbor: The University of Michigan Press and Traverse City: The Petoskey Publishing Company, 2010.

Guthier, Kevin, and Bruce Mueler. *Lake Michigan Rock Picker's Guide*. Ann Arbor: The University of Michigan Press and Traverse City: The Petoskey Publishing Company, 2006.

Guthier, Kevin, and Bruce Mueler. *Lake Superior Rock Picker's Guide*. Ann Arbor: The University of Michigan Press and Traverse City: The Petoskey Publishing Company, 2007.

Lynch, Dan R., and Bob Lynch. *Michigan Rocks & Minerals: A Field Guide to the Great Lake State*. Cambridge, MN: Adventure Publications, Inc. 2010.

Mueller, Bruce, and William H. Wilde. *The Complete Guide to Petoskey Stones*. Ann Arbor: The University of Michigan Press and Traverse City: The Petoskey Publishing Company, 2004.

10 Things You Can Do To Protect the Earth

Save Earth's Natural Resources

The Problem: The human population is growing fast and so are people's demands on the Earth to help us live. The Earth can only reproduce these things so quickly. We need to conserve our natural resources so we do not run out of water, food, and fuel.

1. Save Water. Turn off the faucet while brushing your teeth and you can save up to 1-1½ gallons of water. Taking a shower uses much less energy than filling a bathtub. A shower uses 10-25 gallons of water, while a bathtub uses up to 36 gallons. Even washing your hands and turning off the water as you soap-up, then turning it back on to rinse, is a great way to save water.

2. Save Electricity. Turn off the lights when you leave a room. Remind grown-ups to unplug small equipment like battery chargers for phones and video equipment. They use energy even when they are not plugged into anything. Replace burned-out light bulbs with energy-saving low wattage bulbs. At night, turn off computers.

3. Save Fuel. Heating our homes in the winter and cooling them in the summer, takes lots of energy. Ask parents to raise (in the summer) and lower (in the winter) the thermostat a few degrees. It will save energy and money.

Stop Using Plastic!

Problem: Plastic wraps, containers, and water bottles are polluting our land and water. 90% of plastic bottles are not recycled!

4. Reuse Water Bottles. Fill them with regular tap water.

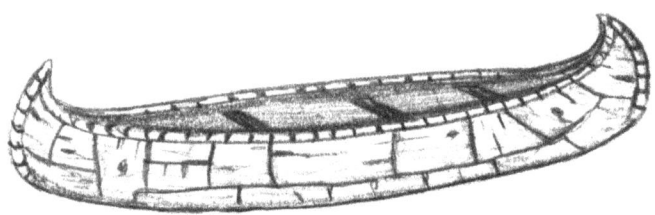

Reduce, Reuse, Recycle!

The Problem: The human population is increasing and so is the amount of things we use and throw away. Earth can't keep up with all of our garbage. We have to start thinking of ways to reduce, reuse, and recycle.

5. Recycle. Talk to your parents about organizing your family trash. Help your family get into the habit of recycling paper, newspapers, cardboard, plastic bottles, cans, aluminum, and glass containers. Make four labels: Aluminum, Paper, Plastic, and Glass. Tape one sign on each of four home trash containers. Start or participate in a school recycling program too!

6. Reuse. A huge amount of paper and plastic is wasted on shopping bags. Ask parents to buy a few cloth bags that you can always use for shopping.

7. Reduce. Ask your parents to start a compost pile in your backyard to reduce garbage. Fruits, vegetables, scraps, and peelings can all be used to fertilize your garden.

Respect Planet Earth and Slow Down Climate Change

Problem: The increase in the Earth's temperature is causing lots of problems for the environment. Planet Earth gives us everything we need to live a happy life. We need to show planet Earth that we are grateful for all that we have!

8. Trees. Ask your parents or school to plant trees. Trees and plants eat up bad gases. The more trees we have, the cleaner the air.

9. Spend Time in Nature. Instead of watching T.V. or playing indoors, enjoy the fresh air outside and our beautiful planet.

10. Tell a Friend. Share this list with a friend. Everyone can make a difference!

Resources

(K= for Kids; P= for Parents; T= for Teachers)

Websites

Children of the Earth – Promotes a greater understanding and respect for animals, plants, water, soil, air and energy systems. Helps children comprehend the positive and negative environmental effects of our actions. http://www.childrenoftheearth.org/ **K, P, T**

Children of the Seventh Fire – Shows what other students are doing to protect and restore the environment in their communities and create peace. www.childrenoftheseventhfire.com/ **K, P, T**

Environmental Education for Kids – EEK! An online magazine for grades four to eight; contains articles and activities about animals, plants, and environmental issues. http://dnr.wi.gov/eek/ **K, T**

EPA: Water Sense Kids – Explores water saving tips for kids at Water Sense! An EPA partnership program. http://www.epa.gov/WaterSense/kids/simpleways.html **K, T**

International Crane Foundation – Works worldwide to conserve cranes and their wetland habitats. https://www.savingcranes.org/ **K, P, T**

Kids for Saving the Earth – Provides an environmental curriculum for all ages that inspires, educates, and empowers children to protect the Earth. www.kidsforsavingearth.org. **K, P, T**

NASA's Climate Kids – Know your world, keep up with the latest, make stuff, play games watch videos, and dream! http://climatekids.nasa.gov/ **K, T**

National Arbor Day – Provides information and resources about planting and caring for trees. www.arborday.org/ **K, P, T**

National Wildlife Federation – Offers fun ways to get kids to experience nature one hour every day! www.greenhour.org **P**

Nature Challenge for Kids – The David Suzuki Foundation website starts with 10 simple ways to protect nature, followed by four challenge activities that offer first-hand experience with the natural world. www.davidsuzuki.org/what-you-can-do/ **K, P, T**

Three Sisters Garden – Provides instruction for planting a Three Sisters Garden. www.kidsgardening.com **K, P, T**

University of Minnesota: An Ojibway Arts in Education Model Program – Combines Ojibway arts and culture with a standard-based curriculum. www.intersectingart.umn.edu **P, T**

Organizations Working to Protect the Great Lakes
(For Parents and Teachers)

Alliance For the Great Lakes – www.greatlakes.org
Clean Water Action Michigan – www.cleanwateraction.org/mi
Great Lakes Echo – www.greatlakesecho.org
Great Lakes Restoration Initiative – www.greatlakesrestoration.us/
Healing Our Waters Coalition – www.healthylakes.org
Sea Grant Michigan – www.miseagrant.umich.edu/
U.S. Environmental Protection Agency (EPA) – www.epa.gov/

Books

Benton-Banai, Edward. *The Mishomis Book: The Voice of the Ojibway.* Hayward: Indian Country Communications, 1998, Print. **K, P, T**

Caduto, Michael J. and Joeseph, Bruchac. *Keepers of the Earth: Native American Stories and Environmental Activities for Children.* Golden: Fulcrum Publishing, 1998, Print. **P, T**

Hart, Lisa. *Children of the Seventh Fire: An Ancient Prophecy for Modern Times.* Granville: The McDonald & Woodward Publishing Company, 2011, Print. **K, P, T**

Jeffers, Susan. *Brother Eagle, Sister Sky: A Message from Chief Seattle.* New York: Dial Books, 1991, Print. **K, P, T**

Kondonassis, Yolanda. *Our House is Round: A Kid's Book about Why Protecting Our Earth Matters.* New York: Skypony Press, 2012, Print. **K, P, T**

Schimmel, Schim. *Dear Children of the Earth: A Letter from Home.* Minnetonka: Cowles Creative Publishing, 1993, Print. **K, P, T**

English Language Arts Standards » Reading Informational Text

Grade 3	
CCSS.ELA-Literacy.RI.3.1	Ask and answer questions to demonstrate understanding of a text, referring explicitly to the text as the basis for the answers.
CCSS.ELA-Literacy.RI.3.3	Describe the relationship between a series of historical events, scientific ideas or concepts, or steps in technical procedures in a text, using language that pertains to time, sequence, and cause/effect.
CCSS.ELA-Literacy.RI.3.7	Use information gained from illustrations (e.g., maps, photographs) and the words in a text to demonstrate understanding of the text (e.g., where, when, why, and how key events occur).
CCSS.ELA-Literacy.RI.3.10	By the end of the year, read and comprehend informational texts, including history/social studies, science, and technical texts, at the high end of the grades 2-3 text complexity band independently and proficiently.
Grade 4	
CCSS.ELA-Literacy.RI.4.1	Refer to details and examples in a text when explaining what the text says explicitly and when drawing inferences from the text.
CCSS.ELA-Literacy.RI.4.3	Explain events, procedures, ideas, or concepts in a historical, scientific, or technical text, including what happened and why, based on specific information in the text.
CCSS.ELA-Literacy.RI.4.10	By the end of year, read and comprehend informational texts, including history/social studies, science, and technical texts, in the grades 4-5 text complexity band proficiently, with scaffolding as needed at the high end of the range.

English Language Arts Standards » Reading Literature	
Grade 3	
CCSS.ELA-Literacy.RL.3.2	Describe characters in a story (e.g., their traits, motivations, or feelings) and explain how their actions contribute to the sequence of events.
CCSS.ELA-Literacy.RL.3.3	Explain how specific aspects of a text's illustrations contribute to what is conveyed by the words in a story (e.g., create mood, emphasize aspects of a character or setting).
CCSS.ELA-Literacy.RL.3.10	By the end of the year, read and comprehend literature, including stories, dramas, and poetry, at the high end of the grades 2-3 text complexity band independently and proficiently.
Grade 4	
CCSS.ELA-Literacy.RL.4.3	Describe in depth a character, setting, or event in a story or drama, drawing on specific details in the text (e.g., a character's thoughts, words, or actions).
CCSS.ELA-Literacy.RL.4.9	Compare and contrast the treatment of similar themes and topics (e.g., opposition of good and evil) and patterns of events (e.g., the quest) in stories, myths, and traditional literature from different cultures.
Source: http://www.corestandards.org/	

About the Artist—David W. Craig

David W. Craig

Born and raised in the state of Washington, David W. Craig grew up surrounded by land as alive as it is beautiful. David began private art lessons at the age of nine. After high school graduation, he pursued his life-long passion and earned a degree in art from Seattle Art Institute.

David has done freelance work for national parks and for various commercial organizations, but currently he focuses full time on his own style of painting. Weaving together story, emotion and moments in time with color and a vibrant sensitivity, each of David's pieces speaks to its viewers in a unique and powerful way. Watercolor, mixed media, sculpturing, and leather work are some of his mediums.

Family ties are strong in the foothills of Mount Rainer where David Craig paints and raises his two young daughters on a rural farm. Enrolled Chippewa (Ojibway), David and his daughters travel throughout the western United States attending tribal gatherings, powwows, and art shows.

About the Author —Carol Trembath

Author Carol Trembath (right) with Josephine Mandamin

BORN AND RAISED IN THE Great Lakes State of Michigan, Carol Trembath has made water a lifelong focus and passion. Her other interest is education. Carol has been a teacher, librarian, and media specialist for over 30 years. She earned Masters Degrees in Library and Information Science from Wayne State University and a Masters in Educational Technology from Michigan State University. However, her initial degree was in English from Western Michigan University and her "first love" is literature. Carol now writes stories that need to be told.

Carol's hope is that readers of *Stepping Stones*, will become more aware of Native wisdom teachings and become involved in recycling and protecting the environment. She has plans for more children's books that will continue Mai's journey to all of the Great Lakes. Her next book, titled *Ripples and Waves*, will retrace the steps of the water walkers as they journey to Lake Huron.

"Water," she said, "is our friend; and if you love something, you take care of it."

Visit her website or Facebook page at: CarolTrembath.com

CPSIA information can be obtained
at www.ICGtesting.com
Printed in the USA
JSHW050221030822
28841JS00002B/39